Codependency
Recovery Guide
41 effective techniques to break the pattern of codependency in relations and reclaim yourself

BY JOSHUA MOORE

By Joshua Moore

FREE DOWNLOAD

INSIGHTFUL GROWTH STRATEGIES FOR YOUR PERSONAL AND PROFESSIONAL SUCCESS!

Sign up here to get a free copy of The Growth Mindset
book and more:
www.frenchnumber.net/growth

2

TABLE OF CONTENTS

—

Foreword

It is my sincere hope that you are able to pick up this book and get a good overview of what codependency is, what it isn't, and how to recognize it. If you see yourself in this book then I hope you can take the suggestions I've put together and apply them to your relationships.

Throughout I will be referring to my friend Jim who is also on a journey of self-discovery and growth from codependency. We will be checking in on him at various points and watch his progress as well as answer the questions he brings up. Look at those conversations as summaries of those chapters.

With that being said, let the journey begin.

Meet Jim

I have a friend we will call, Jim.

He called me one day and asked if I could meet him for coffee.

I had not seen Jim in a very long time and was looking forward to our visit, we had a lot to catch up on.

When I arrived at the coffee shop I saw him waving to me from across the room.

I ordered my coffee, sat down and looked at Jim,

"How's everything been?" I asked.

Jim looked down, his eyes finding something interesting in the woodwork on the floor.

Then he looked up at me with tears in his eyes, "It's good to see you, but that's not…I'm sorry if you thought I was calling to just catch up.

I've got a serious issues that I have to deal with and you were the first person I thought of."

Concerned and somewhat flattered I looked back at him and said "Sure what's going on?"

"Amy and I broke up, again."

"I'm really sorry to hear that.

She seemed like a really nice girl."

"Well she was, but it seems like every

relationship I get into ends the same way.

They keep telling me the same things over and over that I'm doing, I've just gotten to the point where I think there's probably some truth in there that I didn't believe when I was younger.

But as you know, I'm approaching 50.

It's really hard for me to face going into my old age alone."

I told him, "Well first of all 50 isn't old but I understand you want a lasting relationship and things don't seem to be working out.

I get it."

"What do you think is happening?" He asked.

"Am I doing something wrong, something that's sending the signal that I'm not attainable or I'm not worthy of a relationship?"

I've known Jim for years.

He was right, he always seemed to go from one relationship to the other and they always seem to end on the other person's terms.

At first it was easy to say the blame lay with both, or that he was just an innocent victim.

He was such a nice guy and how could people do this to him?

How did he constantly allow it either?

But after the fourth or fifth time, one has to sit

back and say, 'hey something is off here', and that's what I did with Jim.

"Let me ask you something, Jim how was your childhood?"

He began laughing, "Oh are you going to psychoanalyze me now?"

It was my turn to laugh, "No, I am actually going somewhere with this and I want to see if some of the assumptions underlying here are actually true."

"Well I don't think my childhood was any different than anybody else's," he said, taking a long sip of coffee, "I mean, yeah, we had our fair share of yelling and my dad probably drank too much but it seemed like everybody in the neighborhood's parents were like that back then."

I nodded, "Go on," I said.

"I do remember a couple times when my dad hit my mom and that wasn't cool. I hated seeing it.

I remember, you know, little things like that, but we also had a lot of good times in between the not so good ones."

"Okay, I'm not judging anything.

I'm just listening." I said, "You don't need to worry about what I'm thinking or try to justify any of it."

He seemed to relax and then started talking.

"Everything seemed to change when my dad got sick though, it was as if all of the issues that we had before were suddenly shoved off to the side.

He became the focus.

It was all about getting him better and as you know he didn't make it. It was probably another six months after he got diagnosed before he passed."

"I remember it was a tough time for everybody.

I'm sure it was awful for you guys," I said.

"By then I was a little older, so by the time my mom got married again I was already out of the house. Her new marriage didn't last five years.

He was worse than my dad, as far as the drinking went. It was terrible. I felt bad for my little sisters who were still at home. I remember actually coming over and taking them and letting them live with me while I was in college."

"You see Jim, this is why I'm bringing this up. There's a lot of issues here that I think haven't been dealt with right off the bat and I think there's a lot we can talk about right now.

Do you have some time?"

He looked up to me and said, "Right now I've got all the time in the world. I've got no girlfriend and no prospects of a new relationship."

Thus, the seed of this book was born.

The term codependency is nearly everywhere. So much so that it's almost become a cliché, but we all know the clichés are born from truth and this subject hits home with a lot of people.

I know Jim is just one of many who have experienced this painful condition and it is the hope that this book will give you some insight into what codependency is, what it isn't and most importantly how to begin your journey towards recovery.

See you on the inside.

Chapter 1. What Causes Codependency?

Causes

When someone realizes they are codependent or have codependent tendencies, they want to know where they originated. More often than not, codependent behavior is learned in childhood.

This really is not a surprise, as the most impressionable time of our lives is when we are kids.

This is one of the reasons it is so difficult to break these patterns once established without help.

Of course no answer fits every situation, however it usually begins in homes where these traits are passed down through generations. Young children do not have the emotional maturity, life experience, or intellect to deal with what they are experiencing.

If parents are fighting or exhibiting extreme passive aggressive behavior and using the children as pawns it creates a toxic environment. The parents themselves do not know how to deal with their own lives and may not realize they are passing these traits on or that they are failing to provide a secure, nurturing environment.

Families with dysfunction share some common characteristics. These include impossible expectations for the children and or expecting them to do things beyond their capacity or maturity level. This creates a scary and unsafe environment that is unpredictable, chaotic, and unsupportive.

When children are blamed for things, are told 'everything is fine' etc, it is confusing to them because their gut instinct is telling them everything is NOT fine, but it is not being backed up by the adults in their life.

This creates confusion and it also forces them to adopt coping mechanisms to deal with their environment. They may not even realize that they are doing it. They are just trying to make sense of a distorted message from the adults.

So kids believe they are unworthy, not smart, or incapable because of the dysfunction present in their family. This is the root cause of most codependent relationships. Of course, as I mentioned earlier, codependent traits and tendencies can develop as adults and we will discuss how that happens in later chapters. When the parent is not able or unwilling to provide a safe and secure home environment some of the following aspects can begin to happen.

(We will briefly touch on the roles here and go into further depth in the 'Roles in Dysfunctional Families' Chapter)

1. The child becomes the caretaker.

If you do not have a parenting role model, you will take on that role. Perhaps you are the older sibling. You will provide that role for your younger siblings who will look to you because the parents are not available. You do not trust the people that say they love you. You are in pain, so you have a deep distrust and may feel emotionally hurt or abandoned, lied to, threatened and or taken advantage of. If this is the background and the familiar dynamic you understand and accept, you will let your friends, lovers, partners, and family members hurt you into adulthood.

2. You develop a compulsion to people-please.

This happens because you do not want anyone to feel bad. You have an almost pathological need for people to like you and not be upset at you, for any reason whatsoever. You give too much and don't expect anything back. This is how you validate your self-worth and tell yourself you are being fulfilled. When in actuality, what it's doing is creating issues such as anger and resentment later on down the road.

3. Struggle with boundaries.

Nobody has modeled appropriate boundaries for you so you appear weak, meaning you're always care taking, pleasing and taking care of somebody around you or you are too rigid, meaning you're closed off and you can't open up and trust anyone.

4. Guilt is your constant companion.

You may feel guilty about things that you have no business feeling guilty about. You will spend all of your time trying to make your significant other feel better about something, even though you didn't cause it. If you can't fix it then you feel anxious.

5. You can become fearful.

This goes right back to childhood which can be very scary if you're not in a secure environment. You end up having to cope under extremely stressful conditions, which can carry over into adulthood leading to sleeping problems, nightmares, or always being on edge.

Think post dramatic stress disorder in its most severe form.

6. Do not feel like you are worthy or that there is something seriously wrong with you.

If you grow up with the most important people in the world telling you are flawed or something is wrong with you, you will begin to believe it. If it is fortified by being repeated over and over it can be very difficult to get past. You do not really trust people. You have been betrayed, lied to, and hurt repeatedly. The result is it is very difficult for you to form meaningful relationships.

7. You refuse help.

Look, if your needs haven't been met ever and you are the one always giving, when someone tries to return the favor to you, you reject it. You do not feel worthy of the offer. It does not fit the narrative of your life because you are looking to please them. When they try to do the same back to you, you do not feel like you deserve it.

8. You take responsibility for everything, even things that are not your responsibility.

This goes back to childhood and back to the original point where you were forced to take on adult responsibilities. You are looked at as being extremely reliable, punctual, and willing to take on extra tasks. You will also make sure everyone knows you are the most loyal and diligent person there. The problem is it creates trouble for you down the road when you develop resentment towards others for asking you to work extra or pick up the slack of others, even though you don't feel you can say no.

9.You feel very alone.

You thought you had the only family that had these types of problems. We all know that is not true, but it's hard to convince yourself when that's all you know. You are afraid to show your flaws. Also, you would just die if the family secrets were exposed. You can become controlling, because life is better for you when it is predictable. Somehow, someway, you try to control everyone around you. Essentially, it boils down to this, your childhood follows you everywhere and the problems from then manifest in your adult relationships. All of those unresolved issues and crazy out of balance relationship dynamics go with you into your adult relationships.

Are they unsatisfying and or confusing? Yes, but you repeat them because they are familiar.

You do not know what constitutes a healthy relationship, and you feel like you do not deserve one, even if you know what one looks like.

Talking to Jim about the causes of Codependency

Still sitting across from Jim I began talking to him about where codependency got started along with things he could look for in his family history to point towards.

"So you're saying all of this stuff I'm experiencing is due to my childhood?"

"Well, it certainly can play a big part in where you're at currently."

"So does that mean this is permanent?"

"No, of course not and we will get into that later."

"OK, but I don't see myself in all of those people you were describing."

"You don't have to see yourself in all of them, but I'd be willing to bet that you see some of those qualities or they've been pointed out to you in previous relationships."

He paused, then said, "Yeah, you know I hate it when people are mad at me.

I mean, I can't sleep and I obsess about how I can make it up to them."

"It's very easy to become a people pleaser when you have been raised in an environment where it was important to keep things calm."

"Yeah, growing up it was like we were always just waiting around for dad to get mad at mom and then she would take it out on us and it would go downhill from there real fast."

"Not the first time I've heard that." I said.

"And that thing you were talking about with boundaries?

Man, that really hits home too.

I mean I've seen it in my sisters when they get boyfriends, it's like they let the guys walk all over them.

Me?

I guess it depends on the situation but I can go through phases where I let someone in and then get hurt, then other times I never give them a chance to get close.

I'm a mess."

"So, is this making sense then?

The causes are pretty clear to you overall?"

"Oh yeah, they make a lot of sense to me and to be honest I'd never really thought about my childhood that way.

I just knew we had a lot of problems in the house."

Chapter 2. Characteristics of Codependency

Characteristics

The following are characteristics of different types of codependency that you will see.

They fall under the following categories and we will discuss each one at length, "excerpted from codependent no more how to stop controlling others and start caring for yourself" by Melody Beattle.

Caretakers

A lot of codependents exhibit care taking characteristics. They feel an unreasonable responsibility for people who do not want to take care of themselves. If their partner feels bad, they feel bad and feel like they have to do anything and everything to make them feel better, even if they were not responsible for the hurt their partner is feeling. They only feel good if their partner feels good.

It is a compulsion. It is not really to help.

They feel like they need to give you that in order for you to feel better, but in reality what they're doing is trying to make themselves feel better.

This leads to anger, when the help isn't taken or if it doesn't work.

There are all kinds of issues present. The caretaker also tries to anticipate their partners needs, offering and giving help often times before the partner even knows they 'need' it. Constantly obsessing on other's needs can be exhausting. Then they wonder why others do not do the same thing for them. So this leads to resentment and anger.

Codependents may find themselves agreeing to doing things they really do not want to do then take responsibility for the lions share, and then become angry about it because nobody else wants to do it. They do not know what they want or need and if they do know they don't attach any importance to it.

Codependents are caretakers and seek out opportunities to give and feel overwhelming guilt when somebody tries to reciprocate that to them. Not surprisingly, they feel attracted to partners who take without giving back and this is where you find problems with drug abuse and alcohol, and the behavior is essentially encouraged, even if it is complained about.

It isn't surprising that caretakers feel bored, worthless, or empty if they don't have someone to save. So when someone needs help they will abandon everything to come to that person's aid. They will then over-commit themselves to whatever it is they are doing to help that person. On the outside it looks great.

However what they are doing is a compulsion. They feel a pressure to perform and give and give.

They will then point the finger at other people like they are somehow responsible for the predicament of the person they are helping, even though they are the ones that fully committed themselves to help in the first place. In other words they feel victimized, and used, which of course may be true.

But they do not realize that they have allowed this to happen and it is their fault.

I'm not good enough

Another characteristic to look at is low self-worth. There was a lot of dysfunction in a codependent's family, but they will be the first people to tell you there was nothing wrong in their family. Everything was great.

So if everything was great in the family who bears the brunt? They do, they blame themselves for everything that's gone wrong. To them, it could not be any other way.

My parents were mad at me for fighting with my siblings, I was a bad kid etc. Codependents with low self-worth tend to get very angry, defensive and indignant even when others blame them and criticize them for something they regularly do to themselves. Not surprisingly, they will reject complements or praise, but they also get depressed if they are not praised and complemented enough. People with low self-worth and codependents in particular feel different from everyone else around them.

There's a disconnect with the rest of the world. They do not feel like they are a part of what's going on and they are somehow separate from it. They take things very personally and rejection is huge.

It's not something we want to talk about.

If you dig a little bit deep into a low self-worth individual, you'll see that there is usually some sort of abuse in their past. It could be sexual, physical, emotional neglect or abandonment.

They feel they cannot do anything right and are terrified of making mistakes. Not surprisingly, codependents with low self-worth cannot make a decision for the life of them.

They want someone to take care of them. Someone to make decisions so they do not have to. They do not have the confidence in their ability to make a decision and then wonder why nothing is done to their satisfaction. They think their lives aren't worth living.

Low self-worth codependents only feel good when they are helping someone else.

They will internalize the same embarrassment and failure from someone else's failures and problems, especially someone they are helping.

They believe they are not worthy of receiving good things and good things are never going to happen for them. They feel they are essentially unlovable, so they spend all of their time trying to prove they are good enough, and worthy of the validation of others.

Repression

Most codependents are afraid to show the world who they really are. In fact, because they have repressed their true feelings for so long they really do not know who they are or what they think about issues.

Some can appear rigid and controlled. They have compartmentalized their negative feelings about themselves down into a deep abyss where they do not have to deal with them.

They may not even be aware that they are doing this.

Obsession

Not surprisingly, codependents get incredibly anxious about problems and people and they worry and obsess about little things. They are also heavy gossipers. A codependent will lose sleep if they know that someone does not like them or if there is a problem at work they feel responsible for. He or she will internalize it and can't stop thinking about it.

They worry, and they never find the answers. They try in vain to get to the bottom of things, but usually end up going around in circles.

Obviously, this is not a healthy situation, but when a codependent becomes obsessed they focus all their energy on other people and problems and then wonder why they can't get anything done.

Controlling

A lot of codependents feel a need to not allow events to happen naturally. They have to control the entire situation because otherwise it's going to end up disappointing them and making them hurt or sad.

They do not have a healthy outlook on events they have little to no control over.

Perhaps they grew up in a a house full of so much chaos that they were not able to control the events so as they got older they were determined to control everything.

What's interesting is they rarely see it.

They do not see their controlling behavior as a bad thing, simply a part of their mental makeup.

Denial

Not surprisingly, codependents based on their childhood, ignore problems or pretend the situation is not as bad as it looks. Things will be better tomorrow. They work to stay busy and bury their head in the sand so they do not have to think about it. They get confused, depressed, sick a lot of times, and are on medication to control anxiety or they become obsessed with something such as work, spending money, or over eating.

These compulsions can show up in place of the denial as a pressure release valve.

One of the hallmarks of codependency is dependency.

Many codependents do not feel happy, content, or peaceful with themselves on the inside and they seek it out in external relationships. They are hoping that this person that they are getting involved with will provide that feeling of happiness and contentment and they will protect that feeling.

Where does it come from?

It stems from a lack of loving themselves first. What's sad and ultimately distressing for them is that often times they seek out people incapable of loving them back (more about this in our Narcissism chapter).

They equate love with pain because that is what was imprinted on them as children. It isn't that they really want to be with the person, they have a compulsive need to be with that person. They don't take the time to see if that person is actually good for them. Instead they invest everything in the relationship trying to prove to that person that they are the one deserving of love from the other person.

Rather than allowing the person to chase them they make themselves incredibly available and end up with their heart broken time and time again. They look to the relationship to provide all those good feelings they crave and they lose interest in their own lives. They abandon everything, their friends, their hobbies, everything else.

They also don't believe they can take care of themselves.

They need someone there to help them get through everything. That is why they stay in relationships that do not work. They feel they are not worthy of being in a better relationship and do not think that they can find anyone better. They will put up with a lot of different forms of abuse including but not limited to physical, sexual, and verbal.

When they do finally leave that relationship because things got so bad the pattern will just repeat itself and then they wonder why nothing ever works out for them.

I'm sorry for being sorry

Not surprisingly, codependents suffer from a lot of guilt when it comes to trying to have open and honest dialog about issues which affect them. They will blame, threaten, coerce, bribe, advise, try to say what they mean but not really mean it, they will go in circles and back and forth in order to not offend and end up not saying what needed to be said. It turns into a big issue they stress out on before but get nowhere once they do try to talk it out.

They find it very difficult to get to the point because they do not want to offend or upset the person they are talking to, even if it is something they feel is important to discuss. They end up talking too much, then the end up going off topic and maybe gossiping about other people. It is just easier that way. They avoid talking about themselves, their problems, feelings and thoughts. They say everything is their fault and then turn around and say nothing is their fault.

Codependents really do not know what they think because they have been repressing everything they feel and care about in order to sacrifice for that other person. So if asked an opinion on something they don't want to give one until they know what the other person is thinking or what their opinion is.

Lying is very common with codependents with poor communication.

They like to protect themselves or protect the people they love from being offended or hurt.

They also have a really difficult time standing up for themselves and expressing emotions honestly and openly. They believe what they have to say is unimportant and their way of talking shows this.

It's very self-deprecating, degrading, cynical, and they are always apologizing for bothering.

Weak boundaries

Codependents will not tolerate certain behavior out of people, but they will gradually erode those boundaries and do things that they never said they would to ensure the other person does not get upset with them. This happens to a lot of people and boundaries are very, very important. It leaves them open to being hurt and allowing people to keep hurting them and then they wonder why they are hurting so badly (more on this in the Boundary chapter).

Lack of trust

Again, this goes back to childhood.

They do not trust themselves.

They do not trust their own feelings or decisions for other people.

There is a deep anger simmering just underneath the surface. They have carried this with them from flawed relationships in their dysfunctional families over into their current relationships.

They try to put a good face on it and are afraid to face their own feelings or for others to see their anger.

They do not trust themselves to have the right to feel angry, or hurt, or upset.

They will try to justify it and excuse the other person because of an inherent lack of trust in their own judgment. Everything is fine, or so they say, but that anger is just building underneath.

They do everything they can to walk on egg shells and then continue to repress their own anger.

Where does this come from? Being raised in a household where expressing anger was forbidden or frowned upon or not being able to express anger or displeasure in a constructive manner.

Sexual issues

Many codependents feel they are caretakers in the bedroom. They have sex when they don't want to.

They would rather be held and nurtured and loved. But they decide to have sex instead to please their partner. They may endure the physical act of sex, but refuse to enjoy it because they are angry and afraid of losing control.

They have a difficult time asking for what they need in bed.

Eventually this leads to sexual revulsion of their partner. Then they force themselves to have sex anyway.

It is reduced to a technical act. They wonder why

they don't enjoy sex and they lose interest in it and make up reasons to abstain, - headache, anyone?

They end up having affairs because their emotional needs are not being met even if the physical ones are.

Seemingly successful

Many codependents on the outside can seem extremely responsible and or successful. They are the ones that show up to work and take on all the tasks and become upset when others are taking advantage of them. It is an endless cycle of spinning their wheels and they feel like they can't jump off.

Later stages

In the later stages of codependency, many codependents are lethargic, depressed, become withdrawn, isolated, experience a complete loss of daily routine and structure and may feel hopeless.

They abuse and neglect their children and other responsibilities.

Some consider suicide and can become violent.

They can also become emotionally, physically or mentally ill, develop eating disorders and not surprisingly, many can become addicted to alcohol or drugs.

Perhaps you've seen yourself or a loved one on

By Joshua Moore

this list. Perhaps a combination of yourself and others.

Not everyone who exhibits these traits is codependent however, and that needs to be kept in mind.

It is simply a starting point as you begin to develop an awareness of codependency.

Chapter 3. Roles in Dysfunction

Roles

The definitions for codependence can become so broad and convoluted that it seems like almost everybody could be considered codependent in some way shape or form. It gets so diluted that it would be impossible to not fall into one of those categories.   Instead   look   at   codependent relationships as a specific type of dysfunction in that someone helps another (read enables) to underachieve, be irresponsible, lack maturity, be addicted, procrastinate, or encourage or hide mental health issues, etc.

Within the dysfunctional family unit we will see the emergence of roles as a way for children to cope with the chaos and drama.

Human beings are funny creatures.

Because we are social animals we will always try to impose a social structure to make sense of our world.

It falls into very predictable patterns.

Keep in mind that the following characteristics may appear in children and adults that are not codependent.

That's not the assumption to make here, otherwise everyone could be considered codependent.

Rather, look at it like this: When someone is exhibiting codependent tendencies the roles we will discuss below will help us identify this person's place in a codependent relationship.

The roles can be based off of their personalities, birth order, or a combination of factors.

We will discuss the following to gain a better understanding of each one and later we will delve into how to treat them in the healing section.

Keep in mind that these roles can change over time and individuals can also hold more than one role simultaneously.

The Addict

Substance abuse is very common in children from dysfunctional homes including alcohol and drug abuse.

The addict in this role lives in a chaotic state and the way they primarily deal with their life is by escaping.

The physical and psychological dependency becomes so ingrained that they identify and make substance abuse a priority in their lives.

They will lie, cheat, and steal to maintain their addiction.

Within the family unit we see the addict take center stage as everything seems to revolve around them.

It does several things, it gives the family something else to focus on rather than their own internal, individual suffering as well as allowing the other dysfunctional roles to flourish.

The Responsible Child or Hero

This is the child that is older than he or she seems.

They take on a parental role at a very early age.

He or she is very responsible and may look great on the outside.

Usually they are great students, athletes, the prom queen.

This is the child parents look to, to say they are doing a fine job in raising their kids.

The family hero can grow up to be controlling and judgmental.

The judgment can extend to others but they are actually judging themselves just as harshly.

This person may have a lot of material success where you see high incomes, the perfect house etc. They are very competitive and driven.

Unfortunately, this stems from insecurity.

This person, the hero, because of his or her rigid and controlling nature and seeming success that you see on the outside will have a very difficult time admitting that there's even a problem.

Now this isn't to say that all high achievers are codependent.

All I am saying is that if there is dysfunction in a family, then this is one of the role that can appear.

Don't confuse this with somebody that becomes a high achiever because they are driven and they want to find success.

Not every driven and successful person is considered codependent.

The Scapegoat

The next role is the child that acts as the scapegoat for all things.

This is the child that gets in trouble for everything.

Trouble seems to find them even if they are not looking.

What is happening is the child is acting out the anger and frustration that the family is ignoring.

This child provides distraction from the real issues.

He or she gets in trouble at school, that is how they get attention.

The only attention they know is the negative type.

This is the child who grows into the teenager who becomes addicted to drugs, becomes pregnant, or gets the girlfriend pregnant.

The scapegoat is usually the most sensitive and that is why there is so much tremendous hurt inside of them.

They cannot put a name on the dysfunction, they just know there is something wrong in the family.

The scapegoats end of growing up to be very cynical and distrustful with a lot of hatred and can be very self-destructive.

It's safe to say there is probably a lot of overlap with the addict.

This person on the other hand is the one that, because their problems are right there on the surface, may seek help first.

They can be the first one to admit that there is a problem and they are not covering anything up.

Everything is right there in the open.

The Mascot

This child is essentially taking responsibility for the emotional well-being of the family.

The class clown.

The funny one.

They want to divert the family's attention from all of the hurt and the anger and the emotional hardships.

A lot of times, this is the person that distracts the attention from the addict.

This person is valued for their kind heart, their ability to stop everything and listen to their friend when they have a problem.. Incredibly generous.

Their self-identity is centered on helping others so much so that they do not meet their own needs.

This is the person that cannot receive love,only give it.

It is like they do not take on friendships.

Rather, they become the therapist for their friend.

The mascots tend to get into abusive relationships because they are there to save that person.

You will see them become social workers,

therapists, nurses.

In other words, help oriented occupations.

Ruled by guilt and very low self-worth they work hard to never get in arguments with people.

They run their lives by being very agreeable and not wanting to be the bad guy.

This is your quintessential people pleaser.

It is very difficult to overcome this.

It takes a lot of therapy and a lot of self-love for them to come out of this and to understand that it's not their fault, and they are not responsible for everything that goes wrong in other people's lives.

They fit the classic role of the codependent person that is so one-sided and not balanced that they give everything they have and get nothing in return.

The Lost Child

This role tries to disappear.

This is the person that gets lost in fantasy books, plays a lot of video games, watches a lot of movies and TV.

This happens because they do not want to deal with what is going on at home.

They withdraw from from the chaos and deny that there is a problem at all.

So much so that they don't even bother getting angry.

They just withdraw emotionally.

They suffer very low self-esteem and are unable to feel as they get older.

This is the person that does not want to get into a relationship and they have intimacy issues.

These people end up becoming socially isolated.

That is the only way they know how to remain safe and avoid being hurt.

You will see a lot of artists and writers who express themselves through their medium rather than become people that deal with their problems.

At the same time they can hide behind characters or the roles they play.

Again, keep in mind, just because these roles exist does not mean that everyone that is a high achiever is a controller that just because you like to write, doesn't mean you are a lost child.

This is simply a way of identifying roles in a dysfunctional family.

To show that dysfunction is present.

This shows the different roles, if the family is

seeking treatment and looking to classify the roles.

They can be tailored to each one as we move into recovery.

Normal Childhood

What if my childhood was normal?

The question comes up a lot, I get it.

You may not have been raised with an alcoholic or an abusive parent.

However, codependency is passed down from generation to generation.

So even if you live in a home where they didn't do these things perhaps your parents experienced it and they are going to end up modeling that behavior to you.

Example: your dad is not an abusive individual towards you, but perhaps he is a workaholic and is never around.

He is a good dad overall and he is trying but he learned this behavior.

He has learned avoidance as a coping mechanism from his family growing up which can lead to issues down the road for his children.

Or maybe, mom was raised in a home where there was a lot of verbal abuse and she is determined to raise her children in an environment that does not support that.

But perhaps that comes off with a repression of feelings.

I am not saying that this is necessarily something terrible but at the same time it is a learned behavior that she cannot control if she is not aware.

The behavior of repressing feelings is now passed on, maybe not the verbal abuse though.

The fact of the matter is we are all human beings, we all have issues, we all do things that are not perfect.

That's what makes us who we are.

There is no such thing as a perfect family.

So a perfect childhood is not possible.

Nobody is perfect.

You would need not just one but two perfect people working together in perfect unison, all the time in order to prevent bad habits and bad imprinting from mom and dad.

It's okay.

The point is we have to understand and recognize it when we do, then the healing can begin.

Discussing Characteristics of Codependency with Jim

"Whoa, this stuff really hits home for me. I mean I can see all of those roles playing out in my family."

"Like what?" I asked.

"Well, my sister got hooked on Vicodin in high school and it seemed like there was always drama with her and we were always doing everything we could to keep her out of trouble and get her into rehab or something."

"How is she doing now?"

"She ended up going to this rehab place in Arizona but from what I hear she's struggling."

"Sorry to hear that."

"Yeah, it sucks for her kids too and I'm seeing the pattern in them as well."

"How so?"

"Well, her oldest is going into seventh grade and seems to be the one taking care of the two younger ones. She gets them off to school and she gets herself ready. My sister is always bragging about her and what a great kid she is. It's true too, she's a great kid. I feel like I'm talking to an adult when we talk. Poor kid's had to grow up too fast though."

"So the daughter has taken on a care taking

role in the family it looks like."

"Yup, that's what I see there too." He said.

"How do you see yourself in what we talked about?"

"You mean what role did I play?"

"Exactly."

"I guess I was the responsible one. I think because I was the oldest. That's why I feel so much for my niece. It's hard watching what she's going through because the pressure she puts on herself is crazy."

"And you can relate, right?"

"Yup, I can. Also, I remember my little brother was always joking around. Heck, he's still like that, he can't seem to be serious about anything. I always wondered why he was like that, now it makes sense."

"It's funny how predictable the roles we adopt are." I said.

"But I don't want to change who I am, I mean I want to keep my personality the way it is you know, I'm not looking to change my outlooks and all that."

"Look at it this way, you aren't looking to change your personality, that's what makes you unique. See it more as you are looking to become your authentic self, one that is true to who you are. Does that make sense?"

He paused lost in thought. "Yeah, that does make sense. A lot of sense actually."

By Joshua Moore

Chapter 4. What codependency is not

Codependency is not...

Codependency is not caregiving.

A lot of people can confuse the two because the word has been so overused in our lexicon that nearly all examples of kindness and caregiving are looked at as codependent when in fact there is a huge difference. When someone is giving of their heart and for example taking care of a sick parent or child.

There is a big difference because they are giving of themselves to that person because they love them and they want to see them get better.

These are specific situations.

This is not a pattern of relationships and dysfunction that they are getting into and seeking out even if they don't know they are seeking it out on a consistent basis. You can look at it almost as if one is chronic and one is acute.

Even if the acute situation turns into long-term caring. It is not because the caregiver is codependent. They are doing it out of love for a child, a parent or whoever.

It is important to not mistake kindness and love

for codependency.

They are two different things.

Some people are thrust into situations where they have to give of themselves, such as the examples mentioned above, they are not seeking them out but they approach them with love and compassion, kindness, and a genuine giving of themselves to get that person back the way they were.

Look at it this way, codependency is something that a codependent person will seek out because that is all they know.

It is a compulsion to become involved with somebody in that type of relationship where you're going to give everything you have in order to please that person or take care of that person, or control that person.

It is not coming from a place of love.

It is coming from a place of need, because in a way the codependent person is satisfying their own need for acceptance and validation by being involved with this person.

On the other hand, the person that is caregiving is doing is out of genuine love and concern and kindness. They are doing it because they feel compelled to help a loved one, it is not a compulsion.

It is really important to differentiate the two and

understand the difference.   It signifies a healthy response to a loved one in need and not to satisfy their own needs or compulsions.

It is to help and caregive to the one that they love.

The codependence arises from shame. They will deny their own needs and feelings. They have a perfectionist attitude towards helping this person that they are involved with. It is their low self-esteem keeping them around and they have this insatiable need to people-please and feel guilt if they do not act perfect. This is codependency.

The boundaries are just completely out of whack.

The healthy individual, on the other hand, is looking to care for the person. They are doing it out of love. They are doing it out of genuine caring and concern and kindness.

Codependency is a fake proximity of what true love is. It's an obsessive all-consuming need to please, win approval, and validation from others.

Just because you have the feelings of wanting to help others and to be there for your loved ones, that does not make you codependent.

To summarize, codependency is not caring and giving everything we have to people that we love to see them happy or get them through a difficult time. Also, it is not when you are briefly hurt because someone betrayed you, or that we want to see somebody improve and get better because they are acting in a destructive manner.

These are normal reactions.

This is just part of being human.

Chapter 5. Boundaries: What they are and how to establish them

Boundaries

What boundaries are and how to create strong ones

Boundaries are the physical, mental, and emotional lines we draw in the proverbial sand that set us apart from others.

It is how we form our individuality and identity.

Let's put boundaries another way, to paraphrase Mark Manson: Healthy personal boundaries mean you take ownership for your own actions and emotions, while not taking ownership of the actions or emotions of others.

A hallmark of codependence is possessing weak boundaries.

They typically manifest themselves in one of two ways:

The first one is taking excessive responsibility for the emotional well being of another even if they are not (especially if they aren't) responsible for the cause.

The other is someone who expects others to

supply them or to take responsibility for their own emotions or actions.

Healthy people take responsibility for their own actions and emotions. However a codependent suffering from low self-esteem and a lack of self-awareness are often unable to separate themselves from other's thoughts, actions etc.

How do they develop?

Someone with weak boundaries usually comes from a home where there is abuse and dysfunction. The lines have been crossed in an unhealthy manner leaving the codependent with low self-esteem and a lack of knowledge and poor boundaries.

The codependent does not realize that the reason they can't express themselves in an assertive manner can be traced back to childhood and being raised in a dysfunctional environment. If one is ridiculed or punished for when expressing needs then the learned behavior is to shut down and not speak up.

The end result is a belief that your thoughts and beliefs do not matter and this is carried into adulthood and the relationships that form there.

No one is born with healthy boundaries. They need to be developed in a structured family system and taught to us by our families. The codependent however has not had this opportunity.

Therefore in adulthood, they have no boundaries with people, and get walked on and taken advantage of, while others can be very rigid and not let anyone in. If our parents modeled appropriate boundaries then we will do the same, if not then we will model what our parents did.

Someone with weak boundaries is very likely to take on the role of caretaker in a relationship. They will believe that the other person's feelings, wants, and needs are more important than their own.

It is an unconscious way of avoiding their own needs because as a codependent they do not feel the need to tend to themselves or that they deserve it. As expected, the years of weak boundaries and constant giving will create emotional resentment that will build up to a boiling point. Constant focus on caring for others as allowed us to avoid caring for ourselves.

Everything has a way of catching up eventually. Consciously or unconsciously all of the giving we do, there is the expectation of reciprocation.

When it doesn't come, then bitterness sets in. We become upset and angry that we've been taken advantage of.

Signs of Out of Balance Boundaries

• Violating your own needs or wants in order to please someone else

- Giving too much without expecting anything in return

- Continuous taking without giving back

- Allowing others to label you

- Expecting relationships to be the answer to and fulfill all of your needs

- Can't say no to anyone for anything

- Not standing up for yourself

- Allowing someone to take care of you because it fulfills a need

- Falling in and out of love rapidly

- Agreeing to sex with someone so they won't be upset with you

- Inappropriate touching or fondling

How to develop Healthy Boundaries

Establish what you want and what you find wrong with a particular behavior. This is tough by itself for some codependents. When someone is raised in an environment where they are not encouraged to express themselves they will have a difficult time even knowing what they don't want.

Once they do however, then the next step is to figure out what you control and what you don't. For example, you aren't responsible for someone's feelings about you.

You can't control that. Might be tough to admit but true.

Something to keep in mind is this. When you are setting your boundaries, do it when you are not angry.

Don't rationalize or apologize either. Once you've set the boundary you need to honor it and not let your fear or shame take over. Listen to what your body is telling you.

Don't be surprised if this 'new you', who is strengthening and enforcing your new boundaries, is seen as a threat to those closest to you. They may see that you are not putting up with the same abuse that they are used to doling out to you.

Also do it in small steps.

You are not going to change the entire family or relationship dynamic overnight. You need to give yourself time and think in baby steps. Each time you achieve a victory and it strengthens you, you will be able to establish better boundaries until you've reached the point where you are seeing yourself in a different light. Your family, friends, and loved ones will too. It will give you the ability to form your own personal interests and likes. It will give you the ability to have fun where maybe you couldn't see that before.

Don't confuse boundaries with sacrifice

There are times in our lives when there is a call

for sacrifice. However, and this is very important, whatever it is that you consider a sacrifice, it has to come from within you, and you must want to do it. It cannot be a compulsion to help because of some deep seeded need to either be liked or validated.

How do you tell if the motive is pure?

Ask yourself if you stopped doing the activity today would your life be affected?

If the answer is no or are not afraid of the change it would bring, this is a good sign.

If you fear what would happen if you stopped?

Then, it should give you pause.

Chapter 6. The Enmeshed Romantic Relationship

A tangled web

The Enmeshed Romantic Relationship

Romantic love is idolized in the media and looked upon as the ideal for someone to attain.

What's not to love about love? The intoxicating feeling you get from being with that special person. The little dopamine tick that happens when the person texts or calls.

Sure, it's wonderful and something everybody wants.

But is it the best thing for you?

Sometimes referred to as a love addiction or relationship addiction. Patterns emerge involving obsession, compulsion, etc. people in recovery from substance addiction as well as codependents are at a higher risk of developing enmeshed relationships. Essentially they replace one addiction for the other.

So what does an enmeshed relationship look like?

When someone claims they can't live without you or that their life is now complete or 'I'd rather die than go on living without you', on the surface may sound incredibly romantic but could be the signal for a larger problem and should make whoever is receiving this pause and say, 'let's back up here for a second.'

This could be the signal that someone has lost themselves in the relationship and is allowing the relationship to define them. It may be a way for someone to control their partner or to control aspects of the relationship by pleasing and rescuing their partner. The typical codependent patterns we've been talking about in earlier chapters (EliteRehab – MarieM).

Warning signs of an enmeshed romantic relationship

- Isolating yourself in the relationship

- Neglecting other relationships or roles

- Being preoccupied with your partner and the relationship

- Being anxious when separated from partner

- Letting other goals slip

- Depending on the relationship for self-esteem

- Giving up your unique identity for the relationship

- Making the relationship the core of your identity as well as deriving your sense of purpose and meaning from it

Negative Effects of enmeshment

How do you separate a healthy relationship from an enmeshed one? Below are some signs and symptoms to look out for.

• Becoming anxious or distraught when not in a relationship.

Feel like you will never have a meaningful relationship in the future.

• Settling for any relationship to avoid being alone

• Becoming quickly involved with someone before knowing them

• Putting up with abuse in order to not lose your partner

• Violating your standards of behavior in order to be involved with that person

• Jumping into new relationships without getting over the previous one and repeating the process

Intimacy vs Enmeshment

Without an understanding of what a healthy relationship should look like it would be possible to think that all relationships suffer from enmeshment. This obviously isn't the case and as Katie Meilleur points out at her blog it is important to differentiate between enmeshment and intimacy.

Where the former attempts to feel and think as if you are the same person as your partner (you complete me), intimacy on the other hand is knowing someone very well, understanding how they approach things and being aware of differences in opinions, thoughts, approaches etc.

When you are truly intimate with someone you have the freedom to disagree in a safe and secure environment.

Enmeshment on the other hand will not tolerate dissent. Change and growth is not welcome in an enmeshed relationship.

Tips on establishing boundaries in an enmeshed relationship

Rosenberg in his work with helping couples establish effective boundaries lists the following steps to take for meaningful boundaries between couples.

Seek professional help. Having a trained counselor can help you understand your relationship as well as being a neutral third party to help in establishing boundaries.

Set small boundaries. Like an underused muscle the codependent is probably not used to setting or maintaining boundaries. By starting small and working your way up it is possible to gain back your independence.

Here's an example. Let's say a wife wants to go to dinner with a friend. The husband, who may feel like he is being neglected, discusses it with her. They decide together that she will get her time with her girlfriend and that the next week they will get a much needed date night together.

Clear expectations are established and no one is being taken advantage of.

Create your own connections

In the previous example the wife wanted time apart from her husband. This is also important in that it gives her time away from the relationship allowing her to curate her own identity separate from the relationship.

This can apply to solitary pursuits as well. Perhaps the husband is a writer or a painter.

This is something he does apart from the relationship that forges his own unique identity.

Chapter 7. Codependency in the Workplace

Work issues

Codependency doesn't stop at familial and romantic relationships. These are the ones that get the most press coverage however another area we spend a great deal of our time is at our work sites.

Even if you work alone you still have people i.e. your customers that you deal with. It's important to keep in mind that we will still take those same tendencies that get us in trouble romantically into the job. It can backfire spectacularly.

A pretty common question is how can codependency happen in the workplace?

Isn't this reserved for relationships where someone is giving everything they have for the relationship and deriving their identity from it? So how does someone do that in a non-romantic or familial setting?

Joyce McLeod Henley pointed out in her blog the following characteristics to look out for.

Codependents tend to be very good employees.

Why? Because they feel responsible for

everything and that they are the only ones who can get it done right. Or they feel like they can't let their boss down and look for validation by performing at a very high level. There are several behaviors to look for to help identify the codependent in the workplace.

One of the first signs of a codependent worker may come from co-workers. They may complain that the codependent is very demanding of them and can come off as very short or angry.

Why? As previously alluded to, the codependent will feel responsible for everything happening in the workplace even if they are not directly responsible for it. They look at it as their job to make sure everything is completed in a timely manner to their satisfaction and if it doesn't happen?

They can become very resentful. You will see the codependent offering advice that is neither asked for nor wanted. Also, they make implicit statements that management is not doing their jobs adequately.

Another thing to be on the lookout for is a complete meltdown on the part of the codependent. The stress and burnout become too much for them and they can't handle it anymore. A lot of times the employee themselves will come to the boss and let them know they can't do it anymore and need help.

The causes of the meltdown are predictable.

They take on more and more responsibility and feel personally responsible for the outcome.If the work gets behind they try to overcome it by working faster or harder. It is nearly inevitable that they will end up in a meltdown state.

What are some other traits to look for to identify codependents or codependent behavior?

In an interview with Marie-Line Germain she points out some of the tell-tale signs which can range from being over stressed, overworked, overly responsible for work that isn't even their own.

They have a difficult time delegating and feel the need to produce.

As mentioned earlier, their relationships with co-workers can be strained.

They often times feel under appreciated as well.

Does this happen only with employees?

The answer is no.

Everyone wants to be liked. However when it comes to a supervisory role the decisions made will not always be popular. The codependent as a supervisor can face a particularly difficult time trying to balance being nice with having to perform unpleasant tasks such as having to fire someone.

Leaders have to balance empathy with the responsibilities of the job.

Typical problems

When someone such as a codependent struggles with a constant need for validation and approval they can also struggle with feeling like they are being taken advantage of even if they are imposing it on themselves.

There can be a lot of back biting and gossip as a means of coping with the high levels of anxiety they are facing. What this can lead to is a very disruptive worksite where productivity goes down substantially.

Other issues

There are narcissists who can prey on the codependent worker by using him or her to inflate their own sense of self-worth as well as get them to take on tasks they don't want to do. They may also impose their own standards on the codependent that are exceedingly high causing further anxiety.

In nique Pathways, Isabel Einzig shows how to spot Codependency in the workplace and how to deal with it.

• A worker may be overinvolved in helping a coworker with their projects or work

• Feeling responsible for other's problems

• Expecting others to take their advice either solicited or unsolicited and getting irritated and resentful if they don't

---

• Putting way too much energy into solving other's problems

• Taking offence at perceived slights and feeling responsible for another's poor behavior

• Fearing rejection; looking for love and validation

• Working harder than others

• Needing to control projects or people

• Manipulation of others to make them feel guilty

• Always looking for the next crisis

• Looking for needy people

• Expect to be perfect

Steps to take in the workplace

For the employer

• Do not enable other's behavior

• Be assertive

• Do not deal with other's personal problems or issues

• Recognize positive behavior

• Make sure job goals are understood and the expectations are clear

• Document patterns of behavior

• Set boundaries and rely on company policy if

things do no improve

For the Codependent employee

• Set boundaries

• Let go of the need to be the go-to person for everything

• Forgive yourself for feeling bad about not being able to help everyone

• Love yourself first then love others, not the other way around

• Believe in your self worth

• Get professional help – Counselor, therapist, etc

The spillover from home life to work life is real. It is important to understand and recognize if you are codependent in one setting that you are probably codependent in the other setting and you need to recognize it, accept it, then take action to correct it.

Chapter 8. Codependency in Social Media

Social Media Problems

With the average user being on some sort of social media platform on average an hour a day those numbers are telling. It can lead to a whole host of issues and problems.

We will just touch on some of them here.

We all know the person who shares too much of their life on social media. The one who updates everyone on how their boyfriend is cheating on them or they are having a fight with their mom.

Like a window into someone's soul, social media can reveal great insights into the codependent's outlooks, insecurities, and validation seeking behavior. It can also contribute to codependency because it can give an instant response if someone is seeking attention or wants sympathy for something.

They are likely to get it too because the cost for the person giving it is not high. It doesn't take much to like a photo or make a sympathetic comment as a response to someone.

Another way to look at social media is as a giant enabler. How many times have you seen someone 'take up a cause' be it political or otherwise on Facebook or Twitter? What is the ultimate result besides hurt feelings, bruised egos, and damaged real life friendships?

Nothing.

Except that it gives the codependent something else to focus on. To be the caped crusader for justice and to feel really good about themselves at least for a little while. There is no end to the number of causes a codependent can take up either. They can literally go from one pet crisis to the next within a matter of seconds if they are so inclined.

This isn't to say that all social media is bad or anything like that. Simply, that it is another vehicle for people who exhibit codependent traits to tread very lightly around especially if they are in recovery. This platform can easily take the place of a relationship and give the codependent a way to get validation on a continuous basis.

How to deal with social media if you are codependent?

Like anything, the first thing you need to do is recognize that it's a potential problem. Simply acknowledging the fact that social media can impact your life in harmful ways is the first step.

Second, once you recognize the issue you need to control it. For some this will entail cutting it out of their lives completely. For others it will mean severely curtailing its use. You need to see where you fall on the spectrum and be brutally honest with yourself about where you are at.

The following are steps you can take to control your social media and not let it control you: (bustle article -7 ways to stop your social media addiction)

1. Turn off notifications on your phone.

Getting that little icon telling you someone liked your post or made a comment on your soliloquy about our current president gives a little dopamine rush that is very addictive and feeds into the codependent's need for validation.

2. Limit the amount of time you spend in total.

Using a timer or getting a blocking app on your desktop or phone can work wonders. Eventually the need to go on will decrease the less time you spend.

3.Try something new.

A new hobby is a great way to fill the extra time you have now that you are no longer posting or checking social media compulsively. It also creates a 'producer' mindset rather than a 'consumer' mindset. The former is when you are creating something which works in a different area of your brain than when you are simply consuming information.

4. Spend more time with your loved ones.

Nothing replaces in person contact. Sometimes it can be easy to forget that and assume because we see someone everyday on social media that it replaces talking to them in real life. The other thing it does is reduce being distracted and distant from loved ones because you are constantly checking your phone or tablet.

5. Make it something you earn.

In other words look at social media breaks as something you get to do after you are finished with your work. It makes it special for you. You do not take it for granted, you earned your social media time. Also by only checking it occasionally like after you have accomplished something, you will spend less time on it making its lure less powerful.

6. Meet people.

Meeting friends for coffee instead of texting or messaging on Facebook is so much better for your social life. Communication is so much more than verbal or written. Non-verbal cues such as body language can be missed if you are not in front of the person.

7. Just stop.

Delete your accounts, go through the very real withdrawal you will experience and get out there and see what your life is like. I think in time you will see that you will notice the bigger world outside of your screen and automatically find yourself interacting more with those around you.

Chapter 9. Codependency and Narcissism

Narcissism

It is said that narcissism and codependency are like two sides of the same coin. Not surprisingly narcissists and codependents seem to be attracted to each other like moths to a flame.

It is probably one of the biggest issues facing codependents in relationships.

Narcissists can be very manipulative and controlling and when the codependent realizes what is happening they may feel trapped and unable to get out. As a codependent it is important to be able to recognize a narcissist or narcissistic traits. This will help as you begin the journey to healing to avoid them if it all possible, or at least know how to deal with them appropriately.

First, what is a narcissistic personality disorder? This word has become common place in our vocabulary and with good reason. Social media seems to parade this type of behavior to an extreme. Of course people with these tendencies are going to flock to places where they can be seen and admired, either online or offline.

But, what is a Narcissistic Personality Disorder? Taken from the name of Narcissus from Greek mythology, a hunter known for his beauty. Proud with great disdain for those who loved him. Upon discovering a pool where he could observe his reflection he at once fell in love with his image not realizing it was his own. He ended up losing the will to live and died staring at his reflection.

The narcissist is associated with 'a grandiose sense of self-importance, a need for excessive admiration, and a lack of empathy' (DSM-5). Narcissists tend to be very self-centered and are in love with an idealized version of themselves. They are in love with with this image because it allows them to avoid shortcomings in themselves they don't want to acknowledge such as extreme insecurity.

Signs and Symptoms of NPD

Unlike codependency, Narcissistic Personality Disorder (NPD) is classified as a disorder in the Diagnostic Statistical Manual of Mental Disorder (DSM-5).

There are criteria that need to be met in order to make the definitive diagnosis.

• Grandiose sense of self-importance - This is the defining characteristic of narcissism. It is a feeling of being special and somehow singled out for greatness. Narcissists are too good for just average money, relationships, lifestyle, etc. It doesn't matter that they haven't actually done anything to earn this status, they believe they should be seen as extraordinary anyway.

• Have fantasies of power, success, intelligence, attractiveness etc. - These fantasies are supported by fabricated stories extolling their wonderfulness and intellect. The reality is they are hiding the inner emptiness they have and will not tolerate anything that doesn't support this inflated image of their accomplishments, attractiveness, etc. If they are challenged it will be met with rage or coldness.

• Needing continual admiration - Like a never filling cup, the narcissists incessant need for attention and admiration knows no bounds. The narcissist will surround himself with 'yes' men and the codependent is more than ready to serve in that role.

• Sense of entitlement - The narcissist expects preferential treatment and deference from others. Will exploit others without guilt or shame - Narcissits have never developed the ability to walk in someone else's shoes. They lack empathy in other words. People are not individuals to them, they are tools to be used for their own gain.

• A sense of Entitlement - Special people should be treated special. They've earned it in their eyes and expect it. How have they earned it? Just by being wonderful of course, or smart, or attractive. Doesn't matter really. Unwilling or unable to empathize with the feelings of others.

• Pompous and arrogant behavior. It's

pretty easy to see that if you put a narcissist based on the above characteristics with a codependent which we've discussed at length in previous chapters we have the making of something that can only end in disaster if it isn't caught and or dealt with.

Ann Brown writes about how the narcissist will use certain tactics and strategies to shame the codependent into complying with their wishes.

• Shame - Both the codependent and narcissist share the same goal of hiding shame. It forces both to hold onto dysfunctional behaviors.

• Magical Thinking - Or the belief that ones thoughts can influence the world. The codependent will build up the narcissist. He or she is doing this in order to convince themselves (the codependent) that they really are with a great person. Both are working to keep this type of thinking alive.

• Arrogance-The codependent will accept the ridicule and pretend it isn't happening. They become numb to the abuse. Numbness is a very important tool in the codependent's arsenal.

• Envy - The codependent is so beat down that their self-esteem could not possibly see how the narcissist could be envious of anything. Therefore the put downs and minimization of accomplishments is not viewed as envy.

• Entitlement - As a codependent it is part

of their behavior to flatter and aggrandize everything for the narcissist. This feeds into the narcissist's need for validation and praise, thus completing the cycle for the codependent who lives for praising others.

• Exploitation - By ignoring the abuse or being taken advantage of, because the focus is on being liked, the codependent overlooks the exploitation. If pointed out the ability to rationalize, a core codependent skill, comes into play. The exploitation can be financial, emotional, physical, or spiritual. However it manifests itself, the codependent will do everything to overlook it.

• Bad Boundaries - make it very difficult to build self-esteem and confidence. The focus would be taken off of pleasing people and ignoring abuse. With bad boundaries the codependent sees it as their job to make sure their narcissistic partner's needs come first and foremost. It leads to an almost arrogance about how 'good I am' at dealing with difficult people.

Preston Ni lists ten ways to determine if you are in a relationship with a narcissist.

1. Conversation Hoarder.

Of course their favorite subject is...themselves!

2. Conversation Interrupter.

Which leads back to the most important subject that they care about...themselves (seeing a pattern yet?)

3. Rule Breaker.

The narcissist enjoys getting away with whatever they can get away with believing it is their right.

4. Boundary violator. This is typical of narcissistic behavior.

Little to no regard or consideration for other's feelings.

5. False Image Projection.

Narcissists have a compulsion to impress people and don't care if it is real or imagined.

This can include anything from conspicuous consumption such as fancy cars and homes to cosmetic surgery.

Not to say that these items are the sole domain of narcissists, just that they tend to be found here.

6.Entitlement.

Expecting preferential treatment from others whether deserved or otherwise.

7. Charmer.

Very charismatic and persuasive people.

You can feel like the center of the world when they want something from you.

Once they lose interest, they tend to forget about you very quickly.

8. Larger than life personality.

The type of people you see living in beer commercials.

Narcissists see everything they do with an exaggerated sense of self-importance.

The world needs them and or their accomplishments.

9. Negative Emotions.

They may use negative emotions to gain attention, feel powerful and to keep you in check.

However, any perceived slights or insults and they will fly into a rage or forget you ever existed.

10. Manipulation.

Using a romantic partner, child, friend, etc for their own needs.

Example, wanting their child to grow up to be a professional athlete or famous celebrity to satisfy their own ego.

Conclusion

We spent a lot of time going over this section. The reasons I believe are pretty self-evident, codependents like mentioned earlier are drawn to this personality type and narcissists love the unceasing attention they get from codependents. I believe this is one of the most common relationships outside of substance abuse that involves codependence. It is important to be aware of this and once you embark on your healing journey realize that until you have worked out the issues in your own life you may very well continue to attract this personality type.

It is an easy thing to drop back into even if you think you have left it behind. It can creep back into your life before you know it.

Chapter 10. Principles for healing from codependency

12 principles

Dr. Patricia Gorman detailed the following principles to guide you in your journey to recovery from codependency.

1. It takes time to heal. Rome wasn't built in a day and you did not become codependent in a day. It was a period of years in environments that did not encourage proper growth and attitudes to yourself and others. Therefore you need to give the process time to work and you need to trust the process however you go about getting it, i.e. Therapy, 12 Steps, on your own etc.

2. Healing is not a straight line. It doesn't happen all at once and there will be periods where you feel like you are going backwards and or not progressing at all. This is normal and expected. Like learning a new skill, which this most certainly is, you have to expect to go through periods of perceived stagnation. You will have big breakthroughs all at once followed by periods of nothing happening at least on the surface. Fact is the longer we stick with something the more engrained it becomes.

3. Where the mind goes the body goes. By

changing on the inside it will begin to manifest on the outside. Much like improving nutrition will result in a smaller waist size. These codependent coping techniques are going to have to be replaced with new and improved coping techniques and they need to be internalized in order to see them work in your life and in your relationships.

4. Positive Experiences are important. To heal, you need to be active. This means undertaking activities that you can use to calm yourself such as meditation. By using self-reflective exercises such as this you become more self-aware and in touch with your true feelings.

5. Adopt positive attitudes. This is another way of saying fake it til you make it. By adopting the attitudes of a healthy individual and truly experiencing them as if they are your own will give you the ability to change your thinking and adopt healthier outlooks.

6. Take your time. Don't try to do it all at once. You are on a journey to healing and it doesn't have to be done in a day. Like we said in number one, this is going to take time. Enjoy the journey and if something isn't working for you don't worry about it, find something that does. Your individual personality is going to match up better with certain types of therapy than others.

7. Find other ways to express yourself. Other mediums such as writing, music, art etc are great

for building up inner strength and calm. We will talk about one of these in particular in a later chapter that is specifically geared towards writers, but anyone can use it, and can benefit greatly from it.

8. Have fun, exercise, and eat well. This is a big part of recovery. Having a solid exercise and nutrition program in place can do wonders not only for the body but for the mind. Having goals outside of relationships is important and it is a lot of fun to set physical goals in the gym or whatever you use for exercise. Also, getting away from it all and having fun, playing games, getting involved in physical activities like hiking etc can give you greater perspective to life.

9. Stop and smell the roses. Slow down and be in the moment. Being present and not focusing on your past or what can happen if you don't do such and such is a very important aspect of healing. This can be accomplished by meditation or utilizing mindfulness activities.You can even use brushing your teeth as a mindful activity. Being aware of your surroundings and practicing this skill can give someone enormous benefits including decreased blood pressure due to stress.

10. Give your trauma away. Whatever your stance is on prayer it can always help to believe in something greater than yourself. Whether it is a deity or a group it really doesn't matter. Surrendering yourself to it, and trusting it, is what's important. This gives you some distance

between your pain and yourself as she puts it. This gives you the opportunity to process it and heal. Do not underestimate this step.

11. Sometimes medication is the answer. This is especially true for trauma victims, where codependence can flourish, who need a bridge to deal with whatever pain they have experienced. Of course this goes without saying that it needs to be done under the care of a physician or care provider and not down at the liquor store which is a common problem.

12. It is not personal. The changes you experience will not happen in a vacuum. It is going to affect others around you as well, and they may or may not be as receptive to it as you are. It truly depends on the relationship of course, just be ready for any fall out that occurs because you are no longer the same person who started the journey to recovery.

As mentioned in the chapter on 4 steps to Recovery (more in depth in that chapter) it is important to:

1. Accept your codependency. By accepting you are acknowledging a problem and it gives you the impetus to change.

2. Take self-responsibility. Once we realize and accept that others are not able to provide what only we can provide for ourselves, then and only then can we start on the path to recovery.

3. Behave differently. This is the action step. Put into practice what you learn from therapy or wherever you begin your healing. It is only by taking action that you will change.

Reading about and studying are important but there comes a time when you need to put the books down and take the first steps.

Recap with Jim

Jim just sat there.

We had just finished talking and I was thinking about another cup of coffee.

We had waited a week to talk since our last visit.

"What do you think?" I asked.

"This stuff makes a lot of sense to me.

I mean, I especially like the part about this taking time and it doesn't happen in a straight line.

That gives me some hope.

When we talked about people pleasing, I tried to implement some stuff right away and got shot down by my boss."

"Did you start small?"

He laughed, "Nope.

I didn't.

But now I see that it's just a learning experience like everything else."

"That's great you are recognizing it for what it is, and useing it as a learning experience.

You need to be forgiving of yourself."

"Thanks and you're right.

I need to be a little easier on myself.

It's so easy to beat myself up over the little things though.

I'm finally noticing that about myself."

"You've got a lot to offer and when you begin to discover your true self, your authentic personality, just think what you will be able to accomplish.

Use this time as a period of rapid growth as you come out of your codependent ways.

I'm really excited for you."

Chapter 11. Recognizing People Pleasing tendencies

People Pleasing

A hallmark of codependency is the compulsive need to be a people pleaser.

Do you ever find yourself instantly agreeing with someone without really thinking about what you believe or think first? Has your boss asked you to stay late and you agreed even though you had other plans? We have probably all done it at one time or another but for someone with codependent tendencies it happens a lot more frequently than they care to admit.

The following tips will help you first recognize what you are doing and steps to take to stop the practice.

Why should you stop people pleasing? Amy from Strong Inside Out has some poignant remarks that highlight the importance which I've summarized below.

There will always be people who don't like you or approve of you. By being a people pleaser you are trying to control their behavior. Nothing is going to sway them...And it's OK. It is exhausting to try to please everyone and takes away from your productivity as well.

You were not put here for this purpose.

Something insidious happens with people pleasing as well.

You lose your identity.

It becomes this amalgam of saying whatever you think the person you are talking to, wants to hear. It creates a very shallow individual who never gets past the surface level of a conversation. Look at it this way you are robbing others of the authentic you, your voice.

So should you try to be the opposite? Become an arrogant jerk without regard for anyone other than yourself?

I think you know the answer. The key is to find the middle ground.

Some tips from Margarita Tartakovsky at Psychology Today highlight the steps you can begin to take when breaking free from people pleasing.

Realize you have a choice. It is perfectly OK to say no even if it screams from the bottom of your core to not be disagreeable. Sometimes it is the only thing you can do to keep some semblance of a life.

Set your priorities. You need to first know your own values. Sometimes people will ask for things that go against your convictions but you agree to it to avoid confrontation. By having a firm grasp on what you feel and believe, you can avoid these situations and remain true to yourself.

Stall. It may seem counter to our society of instant messaging and social media and it seems like people expect answers instantly, however that isn't the case. Take some time, think about the request, then get back to them. You need to consider the impact on your time and if you agree instantly, you lose that perspective, then find yourself in a time-crunch or worse.

Set a time limit. So you've got past the first step and agreed to help. Now you need to set a limit on how long you'll be able to help. Example, if you are helping someone with moving some furniture. You let them know you will be leaving in exactly one hour. You have set the time limit and they need to respect it.

Don't make up excuses. You're trying not to offend them when you do this, but what happens is they try to find an opening in your excuse to get you to comply or agree. A firm no will take you very far.

Start small. You don't build a house on a weak foundation and it works the same way here. You start small and assert yourself in small situations. As you get better at it you will find it easier to work up to big items such as raises etc.

Don't worry about the fallout. People just aren't that concerned about you. They are already thinking of the next person they want to ask.

People with codependent tendencies however, believe that by saying no to something, they have ruined a friendship. The reality is, it isn't a big deal.

Some questions you can ask yourself

1. How did I become a people pleaser? When you are codependent you have very low self-esteem and you get validation by being helpful to the point of sacrificing yourself.

2. Do other's expectations cause fear? They probably do, because as a codependent you find your identity in living up to other's expectations. It can be a very difficult process to sort through.

3. Why do you keep doing it? It is a compulsion. You aren't doing it from a place of genuine caring, you are people pleasing because you want to control what others think of you.

Here are some signs that you may be a people pleaser (Amy Morin, Psychology Today)

1. You act like you agree with everyone or adopt their outlook to be agreeable

2. You take responsibility for how others feel.

3. You apologize too much

4. You feel a heavy burden by the things you need to get done.

5. You can't say no

6. You feel uncomfortable if someone is angry with you.

7. You adopt the mannerisms of the people around you.

8. You need praise to feel better about yourself.

9. You avoid conflict at all costs

10. You have a hard time expressing your hurt feelings.

This is a very good litmus test to see if you have codependent tendencies. If you start here and really get into the 'why' of your people pleasing ways you will begin to see patterns. Don't just look at the surface reasons. Go a little deeper and get to the heart of the matter. You will be surprised when you begin to see patterns you've never seen before, and begin to understand what is happening.

Realizing you are a people pleaser is a great first step towards healing from codependency.

Recap with Jim

"Man, do I see myself in that," exclaimed Jim as we concluded our talk about people pleasing.

"I really need to take those steps and start making some changes.

One question though, what if I really want to

help someone out?"

"Of course you can help people all I'm pointing out to you is how important it is to know where the help is coming from.

Is it because you truly care about that person or is it because you don't want that person mad at you?"

"Sometimes, I'll be honest here, I don't know."

"That's not unheard of.

You've spent so much time trying to be everything to everybody that you don't know yourself.

Go through the steps we talked about.

It will help you a lot and at the very least make you slow down a little and consider what's being asked of you.

Remember, start small."

"Yeah, I'll do that." He paused then continued, "It's hard seeing things in yourself that you don't like to admit." He said.

"It takes a lot of courage to face things and I think you are taking a huge first step."

"Thanks, I needed to hear that."

Chapter 12. 4 Steps and 8 actions for Recovery

What you can do

As you begin the road to recovery, there are a few things you need to keep at the forefront of your mind.

Before I even begin listing steps, first and foremost you need to love yourself unconditionally.

This is not going to be easy.

You have spent a lifetime trying to make others happy at your own expense.

Now you are being told it is important for you to begin actively loving yourself.

Everything is hinged on this principle.

Get it right and you will find your recovery one of joy and discovery.

Don't do it right away and you will find continuous roadblocks.

Now that we have that established, the following steps are the roadmap of your journey to recovery.

1. Abstinence: The first step towards healing.

It allows you to gain some perspective from the relationship.

You will need this in order to begin establishing your own identity.

This does not necessarily mean a romantic relationship either, it could be a relationship with a substance as well.

Whatever it is, you need to have some distance between you and it.

If it is with a person, then you are going to have to deal with the fallout of that person not being tended to by you, like they are used to.

By no means are we saying this is going to be easy, simply necessary.

2. Awareness. As you get some time away from the relationship you begin to become aware of your self-destructive tendencies and have probably been experiencing for quite some time.

Do not underestimate the importance of this step.

3. Acceptance. When there is some time and or distance between yourself and the relationship you are going to come to a crossroads.

Will you accept what the relationship was?

Do you acknowledge the harm it caused in your life?

We are not placing blame on anyone here including yourself.

It is simply you accepting that there are better alternatives for you out there.

4. Action.   Just like studying for a test, it is imperative that you take this newfound knowledge and begin to apply it.

Simply reading or studying is not enough.

You need to practice by taking action to change your natural tendencies in codependent relationships.

So how do you take action?

What are the steps you take to accomplish this?

Recovery empowers you take back control of your life.

You may have never had control of it and the feelings you are experiencing are probably pretty new to you.

Keep in mind that recovery is not a straight line.

It takes time, practice, and mindfulness.

You are developing self-esteem, and as that improves, you begin to realize the lies you and your family told yourself growing up are simply that, lies. The following action steps will help you clarify your goals and give you a roadmap to follow.

1. Identify relationship patterns that keep repeating themselves and are frustrating you

2. Examine your old belief patterns

3. Begin to set boundaries for yourself.

4. Focus on taking care of yourself

5. Envision yourself in a loving relationship that's perfect for you.

6. Question the self-limiting belief you are holding

7. Be mindful of your critical voice

8. Don't let fear of rejection hold you back – Do it anyway

The goal of healing is to find yourself. That may sound trite and or cliche but it is true. You need to know and love yourself before you can truly give of yourself in a healthy and loving way. It is also true that you will begin to attract others that are looking for the same things in life. You will break the cycle of attracting narcissists and others that take and take and never give anything but grief in return.

Can recovery be a bad thing?

For someone excessively passive in a codependent relationship it is possible for them to go to the opposite extreme and become over assertive and possibly over bearing. An almost hyper-sensitivity to being taken advantage of or taking offense to perceived slights. It is also possible for this person to become selfish and excessively aggressive.

Obviously the goals are not being met, right? What we want as a goal is for the codependent to become a well-balanced individual who is aware of their behavior. Not someone who slips into becoming a narcissist.

This would just mean that the cycle would continue with another extremely passive individual becoming involved with our new narcissistic self. Therapy will help the codependent be able to cope with life in a productive manner. Something else that can happen without proper guidance is that the codependent begins to see themselves as a permanent victim. Everything and everybody is against them and they don't see a way out.

Again, this isn't the goal of therapy.

Becoming aware, then accepting, then taking action. Self-love will breed confidence in this person and allow them to become able to deal with whatever life has to throw at them.

Recap with Jim

"So, what you're saying is all of this stuff I'm dealing with, I can get better?" Jim had an almost desperate tone to his voice when he said it.

Almost pleading.

"Yes, of course. It's a lot of work and I'll start talking to you about some of it, but absolutely, you can recover from the patterns you've experienced."

The look of relief on his face was huge.

It almost seemed like his load lightened just a little.

He sat up straighter and his eyes met mine.

"So what do I have to do?"

I laughed softly.

"There's a lot we are going to be going over, and it's going to take some time, but to begin with, relax."

It was his turn to laugh, "Yeah, that would probably be a good start."

"Trust me, there's a lot but it's good stuff and I think you're going to get a lot out of it."

"I'm just excited that there's help around the corner, that's all."

"You should be, and congratulations for acknowledging there's an issue.

Most people with codependency issues don't even get to this step, the processes and patterns are so ingrained in them."

"Well, I can't go on living like this.

I need to get my life back and I'll do whatever it takes."

Chapter 13. One of the most effective tools for Recovery

Morning Pages

One of the most important steps you can take on your journey to recovery from codependence is to get to know yourself. Your likes, your dislikes, your opinions about life. For many this would seem obvious.

Of course I know myself the would say however for the codependent who has lived their life busily trying to please and not offend anyone and everyone the answers to those questions are not as obvious. You have imposed a systematic squelching of your opinions, likes and dislikes for so long that you probably don't know the authentic you.

So how is it possible to get to know the real, authentic you? The one deep inside of you who knows what you like, what you don't like, and how you truly feel about issues?

Journaling.

Now journaling is mentioned in just about every self-help book out there as an effective means of therapy. With good reason too. It works. Before I get into what the best method of journaling is for the codependent in recovery let's go over some of the reasons why it works.

In an article written by Thai Nguyen he details ten benefits of journaling. I will expand on several of them as they relate to recovery from codependency.

•   Evoking Mindfulness - When you write you enter into a state of mindfulness because you are forced to be in the present moment free from distractions of the past or future. When you write for an extended period your brain enters into a flow state where the words seem to come almost effortlessly. As you write about your struggles or whatever else is bugging you don't be surprised if you begin to see patterns and ultimately answers to your biggest issues.

•   Emotional   Intelligence   -   Especially important for the codependent who has spent years stifling their own voice. Journaling regularly helps to give you your voice back. It will increase your self-awareness and help you to put a label on what you are feeling and why.

•   Healing - Writing expressively is one route to healing - emotionally, physically, and especially psychologically. Stress can cause emotional blockages as well as over thinking, 'what ifs' and 'should haves'. A lot of times the codependent can find themselves going in an endless loop that gets them nowhere except emotionally and physically drained, only to begin the process all over again. Journaling can help to put down in words that you can see and refer back to. It helps to untangle yourself from trauma.

• Self-Confidence - By journaling about positive events or experiences it gives your brain the ability to relive it. You will get a rush of endorphins such as serotonin and dopamine that flood your brain giving you a much needed boost in mood and outlook. Keep doing it on a consistent basis and you will find a catalog of positive events for you to refer back to when you feel down.

So what is the best way to begin journaling?

A process called Morning Pages.

This method was developed for writers to unleash creativity as well as establish the habit of daily writing by author and creativity expert Julia Cameron. What started out as something for fiction writers has evolved into a cultural phenomenon where everyone from stay at home moms all the way to Fortune 500 CEO's use it to clear their mind, get rid of excess mental baggage, create breakthroughs for problems, and learn about themselves. What can work for creating breakthroughs in creativity, which it was designed for initially, was shown to be effective for dealing with all types of issues including trauma and codependent sufferers.

How do you do it? It is called morning pages

because it is performed first thing in the morning, preferably right after you wake up. Julia Cameron says it there is no wrong thing you can write in your journal.

Things that are bugging you, things you hate, that upset you. It all goes in there, just dump it out on the page and get it out of your psyche. The feeling alone of doing a mental dump onto the page, is therapeutic all by itself. While there is no wrong way to write in your journal, Ms.Cameron is very strict about how to do it. She states that it must be performed in the morning.

First thing. She states to do this before the ego can wake up and begin judging what we are writing or as she puts it 'You're trying to catch yourself before your ego's defenses are in place'.

The writing must be done in longhand. Writing in longhand makes you choose your words more deliberately because you naturally will write slower than you can type.

There are people who debate this, and there is a website called 750words that states if you type out seven hundred and fifty words, that is roughly equivalent to writing 3 pages on 8 1/2 by 11 writing paper. Just establishing the habit of writing is probably enough but if you want to be a purist, then follow her recommendation and write it out instead of typing.

As alluded to in the above paragraph, Morning Pages is writing for 3 full pages, no more, no less.

Why 3 pages? In her blog she talks about the process that happens as you write.

The first page is pretty easy overall. This is just the process of getting something down even if it is nonsense. This is easy for a page and a half.

After that it gets a little more difficult, 'but it moves us into action'. She states that anything more than 3 pages and you begin to fall into self-absorption, which is not healthy.

So, 3 pages it is.

To recap, follow these steps everyday and you can expect to begin seeing and noticing changes you never even considered before.

1. Write in a notebook, longhand, first thing in the morning.

2. Write for 3 pages, single spaced until finished.

3. Do it everyday even if (especially if) you don't feel like it.

As a codependent this exercise can prove invaluable as you begin to face issues you may not be comfortable verbalizing but may find writing out a little easier. It also forces you to slow down and really think about the issues you are coming through.

Recap with Jim

"I've been writing everyday in a journal for the past week and it is amazing." Said Jim.

"Really, how so?

What have you noticed?"

"Well, at first when I started I found that my mind kept wandering and I was focused on my hand hurting from holding the pen but I was determined to keep writing because of the benefits you were talking about."

"And?"

"It was weird, after a while, say the third day of doing it, I was finding myself really looking forward to my writing session.

It was as if I got rid of all this garbage out of my mind and I felt more clear headed the rest of the day.

I didn't find myself obsessing over my breakup or feeling the guilt I'd felt for not changing enough for her.

It was like it was all left on the paper in my notebook."

"That's really great to hear.

I am so glad you're getting some good use out of it.

Just wait until I give you the next tool when we

meet next week.

I think you'll really like it coupled with this."

"Now you've got me curious." He said with a chuckle.

By Joshua Moore

Chapter 14. Developing a Mindfulness Practice

Mindfulness

An overused word in today's lexicon is mindfulness.

Used, but is it really understood? There seems to be a new app released everyday that is supposed to help you become more mindful and focused on the present. Not a bad thing obviously but it seems to fall into the category of something else to master and get good at.

In his book 'The Practicing Mind' Thomas Sterner describes today's frantic pace and all of the racing thoughts we keep in our mind as to a chariot driver without reins. The horses will run wild leaving us exhausted and overwhelmed by everything. Sterner looks at life as a series of practice sessions. With his background in music this is appropriate. It helped him to develop skills in other areas such as golf.

What does this have to do with codependency?

A lot of the behavior exhibited by the codependent is habitual.

You may find yourself slipping into the same old patterns, just it is now with new people.

By becoming mindful of your thoughts and actions, as well as what you are allowing others to do to you, and peering at them without the prism of codependence, you can begin to see problems you have been overlooking for far too long. By approaching this as practice you take the judgment out of the equation and instead begin to correct the steps and thought patterns that got you there in the first place.

Sterner uses the example, if you had 3 balls and you were trying to throw them in a wastebasket near your desk how would you approach it? Would you throw one at the basket, and if it didn't make it, get mad and say 'you just aren't cut out for making baskets'?

Probably not.

You would adjust your aim a little and shoot the next one, more than likely getting a little closer. You would then take your last shot and the chances of making it have increased quite a bit because you had the practice shots before hand. What if you took that same attitude towards your recovery? Instead of saying you just aren't cut out for recovery, and are far too damaged, why not begin taking small steps in the right direction? This is where mindfulness comes into play. You can call it meditation, or just being still, but allowing yourself to sit and try to not think is a worthy endeavor.

I should also mention that it is incredibly

difficult.

Try it sometime. Sit down in a quiet room and just sit there. Within seconds your brain, which is so used to constant stimulation, will begin to revolt. It will talk to you about how dumb it is to sit there and you should be 'doing' something else.

Don't judge yourself though. Don't worry that you can't be still. It is normal and in time you will find that you are able to quiet your mind. Eventually you will be able to sit for longer periods and find an increase in harmony inside.

Your stress level will drop and you will find yourself centered. The focus is no longer on external forces such as unhealthy relationships or other compulsions.

Science backs this up too.

Mindfulness affects the physical structure of the brain.

As detailed by Catherine Hambley, PhD in The Benefits to Developing a Mindfulness Practice, developing a mindfulness routine will have the following affects on the brain:

• The amygdala, the area that's responsible for our stress response, will begin to atrophy or get smaller.

• The hippocampus, in charge of learning and memory processing thickens (this is a good thing)

• The pre-frontal cortex gets bigger which improves thinking, decision-making, focus, and emotional regulation.

• The connections between the amygdala (responsible for our stress response) and other areas of the brain become weaker, while other areas associated with attention and concentration get stronger.

What are some benefits you will experience? The same article details them below.

• More time spent in the present mode vs thinking about the past or future. This is important because when you are living in the past or future it is because you are discontent with the present state of your life (usually).

• Mindfulness takes the focus off of you and helps you become more empathetic and compassionate. This may sound counter-intuitive but it isn't. Codependence is not really just about being focused on another person's needs although that plays a part, the compulsion to put other's needs above your own comes from your own need for validation etc.

• Decreased tendency to judge other including ourselves.

• Improved emotional regulation.

• Improved thinking, planning, and decision

making. We are less reactive to external events.

So how do we go about setting up our mindfulness practice? It really isn't difficult. Do the following and above all be patient with yourself.

• Find a place without interruptions and begin to focus on your breath. Breathing in and out through your nose.

• Keep your attention on your breath during both inhalation and exhalation.

• When your mind wanders (and it will) gently bring the focus back to your breath.

• Just observe your thoughts, do not judge them.

• Start with ten minutes per day and build up to however long you want - usually in the 20-30 minute range will yield amazing benefits.

The most important thing to realize when you start this is to not judge yourself. It's very important. Don't think of this as something you 'get good at'.

It isn't designed to be mastered.

It is a tool to help you in your recovery.

Within a month's time you will see positive changes and coupled with your Morning Pages you will become unstoppable.

Use it and benefit.

Recap with Jim

"OK, I have to say this one was tougher to implement than the journaling.

It's weird too because I thought it was going to be easy."

I laughed, "Everyone thinks that until they try it.

What did you find difficult?"

"I sat down and tried to be still, you know, just empty my mind but as soon as I tried, I felt like I had an avalanche of thoughts flooding me, some were good, some were not so good, and some were just weird."

"Like pink elephants."

"What does that mean?" he asked.

"When someone says not to think about pink elephants what's the first thing you think of?"

"Pink elephants." He said with a laugh.

"Exactly.

So, did you stick with it?"

"I did.

After reading more about it I could see there are definitely some benefits to be gained.

So, I stuck or am sticking with it.

I sit down in the morning before work and

before I even write in my journal.

I've found the more I do it, the easier it gets.

I'm sitting there and just letting myself be still.

I concentrate on my breathing and feel myself relax after a few minutes.

Lately, I've noticed some really good breakthroughs when I do this first then write in my journal."

"That's a great way to go about it."

Chapter 15. Tips for leading a well-balanced life

Tips and advice

So we've looked at journaling and creating a mindfulness practice but how do you put it all together?

You have to find time to incorporate these changes into your routine and it can be difficult.

Anything that requires change can be though. It boils down to how bad do you want to see positive changes into your life.

It starts with your mindset.

Do you view your recovery as a one and done ordeal that you need to get through? If you do, I can assure you that it will be a very tough road for you.

Recovery is an ongoing activity and needs to be incorporated as such. It's like either going on a diet because you've put on a few pounds and you want to lose them or you've been diagnosed with diabetes and heart disease and the doctor is telling you that if you don't make the changes you will die within a year?

Which one imparts more urgency? Well, with

recovery you need to approach it the same way.

There is an urgency to your recovery that needs to be realized. Once you do this the rest will begin to fall into place.

So with the mindset firmly entrenched that change is a good thing and necessary for your recovery you can now look at the following tips to create a framework for you. Keep in mind that not all of these tips will just apply to codependency. The point of leading a well balanced life is just that.

This is for you to undertake to improve yourself and in the process of doing so you will find that other issues begin to improve as well. Consider it a holistic view of healing.

• Journal every day. Use the Morning Pages template if that works for you or not but get those thoughts and feelings down on paper or your computer screen everyday.

• Practice mindfulness or meditation everyday. Work up to 20 minutes per day and see where you're at. This will help develop a 'present' perspective where you are in the place you should be at all times.

• Pay attention to your health. Eat right and exercise. You will get that necessary rush of endorphins from the exercise and eating correctly will give you increased energy as well. That's a gift that keeps on giving.

• Get enough sleep. It can't be overstated how important it is to get a full 8 hours of sleep every night even if it means turning the TV off an hour earlier.

• Practice good sleep hygiene. Dovetailing with the point above, make sure you sleep in an environment conducive to sleeping well such as turning off tablets or keeping them out of your room, making sure the room is cool, going to sleep at roughly the same time every night etc. You can find lots of information out there regarding this subject.

• Nurture healthy relationships. Seek out relationships that build you up and help you. Not the kind you are used to where you are torn down and taken advantage of. Of course this isn't everything but that isn't the point. What it does though is give you a start. You will begin to make your own schedule and not have to worry about looking up the top ten ways to ...fill in the blank.

This is your life and you are the author of it. It is time to take it back and experience all life has to offer you.

You may find that you end up going back to school because you have courage to step out of your comfort zone and have decided what you really want is now within reach if you take the steps.

It's a time to be excited for the future.

You are getting yourself into a place where good things are happening for you and you should be excited about them.

Set the framework and begin creating the life you want for yourself, not one based off of the wants and needs of another person.

Life isn't meant to be lived that way.

Chapter 16. What does a healthy Relationship look like?

A Healthy Relationship

First of all, realize I did not ask 'What does a perfect relationship look like'.

That does not exist.

However, it is possible to have a healthy one when two committed partners work on it together. What do you look for in one then? Healthy relationships are a lot of work but it can be good work and very rewarding.

Kelsey Borresen in the Huffington Post detailed 9 things to look for:

1. Have a realistic expectation about love. This cuts right to the quick with someone codependent who is addicted to 'being in love'. The reality is relationships change over time and it is OK. Working together to overcome them is a sign of a healthy relationship.

2. You don't take minor issues personally. This does not mean however that you allow yourself to be walked on or taken advantage of. Everyone makes mistakes and slips up at times.

3. You consider yourself on the same team.

4. You take ownership rather than shift blame.

Again, this is an area for the person with codependency issues to be careful. Take responsibility for your own actions, not those of your partner.

5. You have trust in the relationship which gives you security.

6. You help each other out. This is not a one way street though. If it seems like the balance is shifting it is time to reevaluate.

7. Able to talk about uncomfortable subjects. It can range from money to sex, nothing is off limits. This can be difficult for the codependent to come to grips with.

8. You are not threatened by your partner's growth and vice versa. People change and it is OK. Encouraging new hobbies or interests even if the other isn't particularly interested in pursuing it. It gives much needed space between the two.

9. Fight fair. This goes without saying but mutual respect and the ability to keep things in perspective is very important.

John Kim in Psychology Today has some good points as well.

He states that healthy love requires separate containers. This means having separate lives coming together to share their lives with each other. It is not spending every waking moment with each other and becoming romantically enmeshed. 'Healthy love requires facing in the same direction.

Not at each other.'

What this means is living your lives together and facing things together but not for each other. This will put you right back into the codependent traits we saw before in previous relationships. He further states that passion, attraction and chemistry come from one place - trust.

Without trust there is no way to have the other things mentioned above. Healthy relationships are not built on powerful feelings. Simply put, they are built from the ground up and nurtured and cared for.

Chapter 17. Other Resources to look into

Other options

No book about recognizing and treating codependency would be complete without a resource guide for you to look into. Generally therapy consists of either some sort of individual counseling or group therapy.

It depends on the individual and his or her preferences. I think the best approach is to go through the steps outlined in the recovery section of this book first.

Go through the steps of Abstinence, Awareness, Acceptance, and Action. Then begin some type of mindfulness practice and journaling. This will put you on the right path and when you do go for outside help you will have already begun, and taken responsibility for, the process of your own healing which is very important.

Here are some resources courtesy of Lisa Hann at Sober Nation:

• Individual Counseling - Probably the most effective way of dealing with codependency. You will look at the underlying causes and with the help of a trained professional be able to work through them. You can get help finding a counselor by calling 1-800-662-HELP or by going to their website - SAMHSA.gov

• Co-Dependents Anonymous - This is similar to Alcoholics Anonymous. On their website (CoDA.org) you will find many resources including helpful reading material. The website will also point out local chapter meetings for you as well. Meeting other people who are going through the same issues as you can be very empowering.

• Al-Anon/Alateen - Primarily intended for the families of alcoholics. It is modeled on the 12 step program and is another way to find people who are going through similar circumstances and have codependent issues.

• Residential Treatment - Codependency is treated just like addiction and at times in extreme cases a residential treatment option can be appropriate.

Conclusion

Final Thoughts

We have covered a lot of ground in this book. From looking at the causes of codependency all the way to how to begin the journey to recovery. Look at the end of this book as the beginning of your healing.

The suggestions are backed by science and have been proved time and time again.

Own your own recovery.

It is probably not what you are used to if you've been in a codependent relationship for a while. You are used to taking care of others and neglecting your self-care.

Now is the time to take back your life and begin living it for you on your terms.

When you can see what life has to offer, and that you are a special and unique person put on this earth to contribute, you will see just how important your recovery is not just to you, but to the world.

Does that sound melodramatic?

I admit it may sound that way but it isn't. I assure you.

What you have to contribute is necessary even if

it does not seem big in your eyes.

Do not underestimate your impact.

By Joshua Moore

FREE DOWNLOAD

INSIGHTFUL GROWTH STRATEGIES FOR YOUR PERSONAL AND PROFESSIONAL SUCCESS!

Sign up here to get a free copy of The Growth Mindset book and more:
www.frenchnumber.net/growth

You may also like...
EMOTIONAL INTELLIGENCE SPECTRUM
EXPLORE YOUR EMOTIONS AND IMPROVE YOUR
INTRAPERSONAL INTELLIGENCE
BY JOSHUA MOORE AND HELEN GLASGOW

Emotional Intelligence Spectrum is the one book you need to buy if you've been curious about Emotional Intelligence, how it affects you personally, how to interpret EI in others and how to utilize Emotional Quotient in every aspect of your life.

Once you understand how EQ works, by taking a simple test, which is included in this guide, you will learn to harness the power of Emotional Intelligence and use it to further your career as you learn how to connect with people better.

You may also like...
I AM AN EMPATH
ENERGY HEALING GUIDE FOR EMPATHIC AND
HIGHLY SENSITIVE PEOPLE
BY JOSHUA MOORE

Am an Empath is an empathy guide on managing emotional anxiety, coping with being over emotional and using intuition to benefit from this sensitivity in your everyday life – the problems highly sensitive people normally face.

Through recongnizing how to control emotions you have the potential to make the most of being in tune with your emotions and understanding the feelings of people around you.
Begin your journey to a fulfilling life of awareness and support today!

You may also like...
MAKE ROOM FOR MINIMALISM
A PRACTICAL GUIDE TO SIMPLE AND
SUSTAINABLE LIVING
BY JOSHUA MOORE

Make Room for Minimalism is a clear cut yet powerful, step-by-step introduction to minimalism, a sustainable lifestyle that will enable you to finally clear away all the physical, mental and spiritual clutter that fills many of our current stress filled lives. Minimalism will help you redefine what is truly meaningful in your life.

Eager to experience the world of minimalism?
Add a single copy of **Make Room for Minimalism** to your library now, and start counting the books you will no longer need!

F№

Presented by French Number Publishing
French Number Publishing is an independent
publishing house headquartered in Paris, France
with offices in North America, Europe, and Asia.
F№ is committed to connect the most promising
writers to readers from all around the world.
Together we aim to explore the most challenging
issues on a large variety of topics that are of
interest to the modern society.

F№

By Joshua Moore

Made in the USA
Columbia, SC
22 January 2019